# High-Frequency Words

## Words LEVEL A

### Stories & Activities

Editorial Development: Joy Evans
Lisa Vitarisi Mathews
Camille Liscinsky
Copy Editing: Cathy Harber
Carrie Gwynne
Art Direction: Cheryl Puckett
Cover Design: Liliana Potigian
Illustration: Ann Iosa
Design/Production: Olivia C. Trinidad
Arynne Elfenbein

EMC 3376

**Evan-Moor**
EDUCATIONAL PUBLISHERS
*Helping Children Learn since 1979*

**Congratulations on your purchase of some of the finest teaching materials in the world.**

**Correlated to State Standards**

*Photocopying the pages in this book is permitted for single-classroom use only. Making photocopies for additional classes or schools is prohibited.*

For information about other Evan-Moor products, call 1-800-777-4362, fax 1-800-777-4332, or visit our Web site, www.evan-moor.com. Entire contents © 2008 EVAN-MOOR CORP. 18 Lower Ragsdale Drive, Monterey, CA 93940-5746. Printed in USA.

Visit *teaching-standards.com* to view a correlation of this book's activities to your state's standards. This is a free service.

CPSIA: Media Lithographics, 6080 Triangle Drive, City of Commerce, CA USA. 90040 [3/2010]

# Contents

# What's in This Book?

High-frequency words are the words that readers encounter most often in reading materials. The ability to read these high-frequency words is necessary for fluent reading. Since many high-frequency words are not phonetic, students need repeated practice to recognize the words on sight. The stories and activities in this book help students read 100 Dolch high-frequency words quickly and accurately.

## 15 Pretests

Use the pretests to determine which words a student needs to master. Each pretest corresponds to the high-frequency words introduced in the same-numbered unit.

## 15 Units

### Learn New Words

On this page, students are introduced to the high-frequency words that are the unit's focus. You may wish to follow these steps to present each word:

- Point to the word, say the word, and use it in a sentence.

- Have students read the word, and then point to each letter as they spell the word aloud.

- Ask students to write the word twice, spelling the word aloud as they write it.

- At the bottom of the page, have students point to and read each word once again.

### Practice New Words

Fun activities, presented in a variety of formats, give students practice in reading the unit's high-frequency words. Students may work independently or as a group.

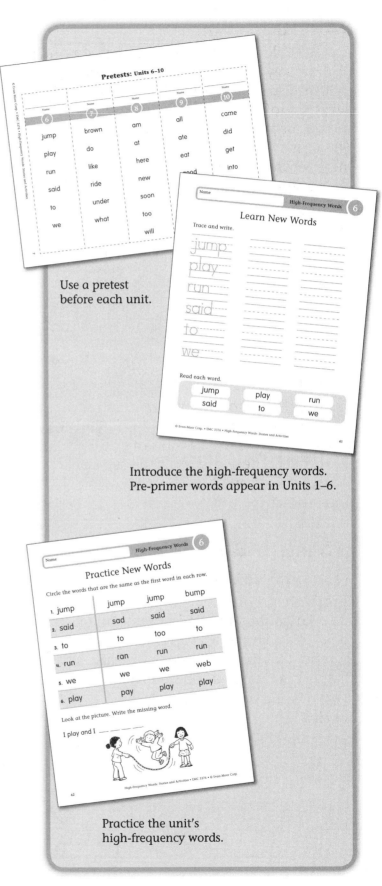

Use a pretest before each unit.

Introduce the high-frequency words. Pre-primer words appear in Units 1–6.

Practice the unit's high-frequency words.

## Read Naming Words

A picture dictionary introduces 2 to 4 nouns that are key to reading the story that follows. These nouns are taken from the Dolch list of 95 nouns. Students encounter the nouns individually and then in context. The unit's high-frequency words are also incorporated into the activities on the page, giving students further practice and review.

## Story

The story is the unit's culminating activity. Students read the unit's high-frequency words and key story vocabulary in a meaningful context. Story vocabulary is carefully controlled, so students encounter only those words they have learned.

## Word-List Slider

The slider is a wonderful tool to help students master reading the high-frequency words and key story vocabulary quickly and accurately. The slider may be used at any step in the lesson. And it is perfect for home practice!

## Additional Resources

### 3 Cumulative Tests

Cumulative word lists follow every fifth unit. These may be used as assessment tools. Have students keep track of the number of words they read correctly. The lists also make great home practice.

### Award

A reproducible certificate acknowledges the accomplishment of reading 100 high-frequency sight words.

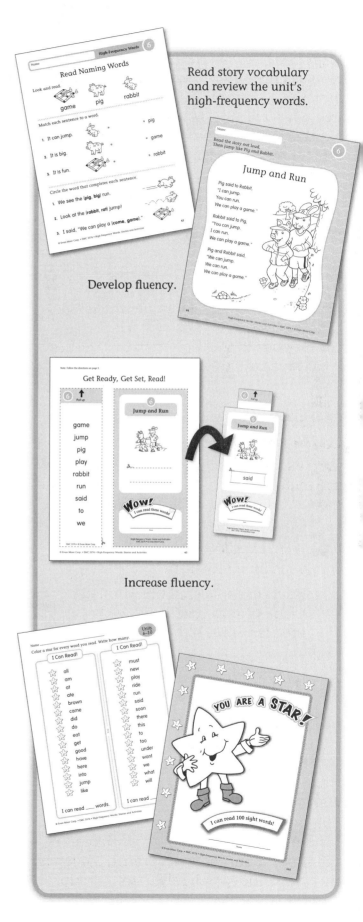

Read story vocabulary and review the unit's high-frequency words.

Develop fluency.

Increase fluency.

# Pretests: Units 1–5

Name

**1**

A  a

find

I

little

see

two

you

---

Name

**2**

can

help

in

look

me

the

up

---

Name

**3**

away

big

come

down

go

not

---

Name

**4**

blue

for

is

my

red

where

yellow

---

Name

**5**

and

funny

it

make

one

three

# Pretests: Units 6–10

| | | | | |
|---|---|---|---|---|
| **Name** | **Name** | **Name** | **Name** | **Name** |
| **(6)** | **(7)** | **(8)** | **(9)** | **(10)** |
| jump | brown | am | all | came |
| play | do | at | ate | did |
| run | like | here | eat | get |
| said | ride | new | good | into |
| to | under | soon | have | there |
| we | what | too | must | this |
| | | will | want | |

# Pretests: Units 11–15

Name

**11**

but

four

now

say

they

was

who

**12**

black

gray

hi

on

our

out

white

**13**

he

pink

purple

saw

she

that

with

**14**

are

good-bye

green

hello

orange

pretty

so

**15**

be

no

please

ran

well

went

yes

High-Frequency Words: Stories and Activities • EMC 3376 • © Evan-Moor Corp.

# Learn New Words

Trace and write.

A a

find

I

little

see

two

you

Read each word.

| A a | find | I | little |
|---|---|---|---|

| see | two | you |
|---|---|---|

# Practice New Words

Circle the words that are the same as the first word in each row.

| | | | |
|---|---|---|---|
| 1. find | find | find | fin |
| 2. two | too | two | two |
| 3. little | little | lip | little |
| 4. you | you | you | yell |
| 5. see | saw | see | see |
| 6. I | I | L | I |
| 7. a | b | a | a |

Trace and read.

I see you.

# Read Naming Words

Look and read.

baby

feet

Circle the pictures that go with each word.

1. feet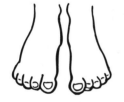

2. baby

Circle the word that completes each sentence.

1. I see (**feet**, **baby**).

2. I see a (**feet**, **baby**).

Name

Read the story out loud.
Color two little feet.

# A Little Baby

I see a little baby!
I see two little feet!

You find a baby.
You find feet.

I see a little baby!
I see two little feet!

You find a baby.
You find feet.

Note: Follow the directions on page 5.

# Get Ready, Get Set, Read!

# A Little Baby

# Learn New Words

Trace and write.

can

help

in

look

me

the

up

Read each word.

| can | help | in | look |
|-----|------|-----|------|

| me | the | up |
|----|-----|-----|

# Practice New Words

Connect to make a match.

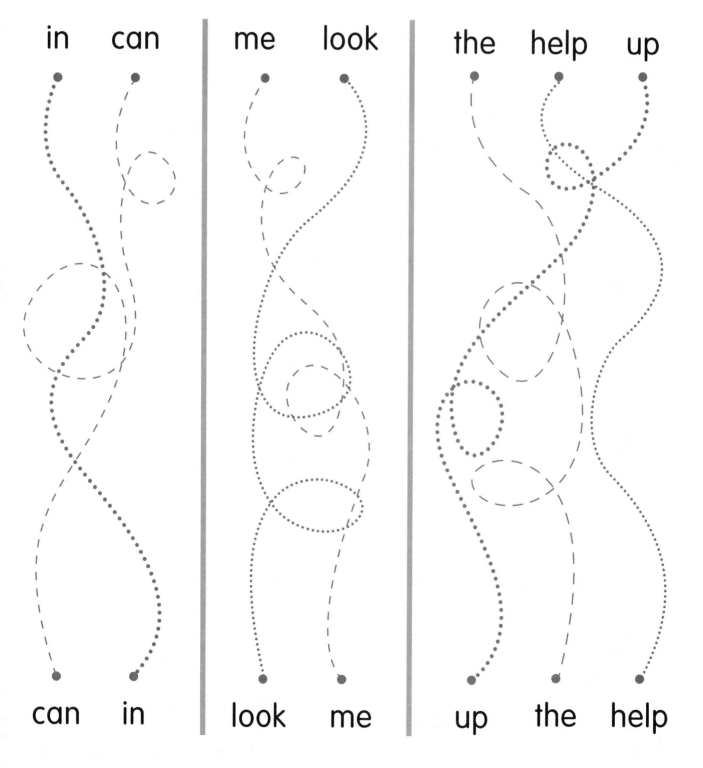

in    can       me    look       the    help    up

can    in       look    me       up    the    help

High-Frequency Words: Stories and Activities • EMC 3376 • © Evan-Moor Corp.

# Read Naming Words

Look and read.

apple

tree

Draw lines to match the words with the pictures.

1. tree •

2. apple •

Circle the word that completes each sentence.

1. I see the (**apple**, **tree**).

2. Can you see the (**apple**, **tree**)?

Read the story out loud.
Color two apples.

# Help Me!

Help!

Look up!

Look up in the apple tree.

Can you see me?

Help!

Look up!

Look up in the apple tree.

Can you help me?

Help!

Look up!

See me in the apple tree.

You can help me.

High-Frequency Words: Stories and Activities • EMC 3376 • © Evan-Moor Corp.

Note: Follow the directions on page 5.

# Get Ready, Get Set, Read!

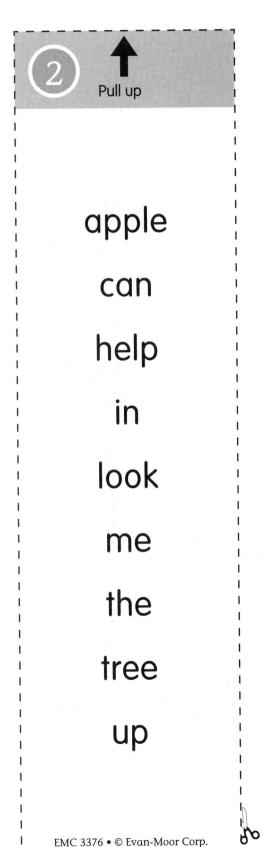

# Help Me!

# Learn New Words

Trace and write.

away

big

come

down

go

not

Read each word.

| away | big | come |
|------|-----|------|
| down | go | not |

# Practice New Words

Circle the words that are the same as the first word in each row.

| | | | |
|---|---|---|---|
| 1. not | the | not | not |
| 2. big | big | bag | big |
| 3. go | go | to | go |
| 4. away | away | away | way |
| 5. come | come | came | come |
| 6. down | brown | down | down |

Trace and read.

1. Go away!

2. Come down.

# Read Naming Words

Look and read.

bird          dog          tree

Circle the pictures that go with each word.

**1.** dog

**2.** tree

**3.** bird

Draw a dog.                 Draw a bird in a tree.

Read the story out loud.
Color the big dog.

# Go Away!

Go away!
Go away, big dog!
You can not go up.
You can not go up the tree.

Come down, little bird.
Come down the tree.
Come down, little bird.
Come see me.

 High-Frequency Words: Stories and Activities • EMC 3376 • © Evan-Moor Corp.

Note: Follow the directions on page 5.

# Get Ready, Get Set, Read!

away

big

bird

come

dog

down

go

not

tree

• EMC 3376 • High-Frequency Words: Stories and Activities     25

**Go Away!**

# Learn New Words

Trace and write.

blue

for

is

my

red

where

yellow

Read each word.

| blue | for | is | my |
| --- | --- | --- | --- |
| red | where | yellow | |

Name

# Practice New Words

Are the words the same? Color the face.

| | | | yes | no |
|---|---|---|---|---|
| 1. | red | read | ☺ | ☹ |
| 2. | where | were | ☺ | ☹ |
| 3. | blue | blue | ☺ | ☹ |
| 4. | my | my | ☺ | ☹ |
| 5. | is | it | ☺ | ☹ |
| 6. | for | far | ☺ | ☹ |
| 7. | yellow | yellow | ☺ | ☹ |

Complete the sentences. Use the words in the box.

for   my

1. The apple is ___ ___ ___ you.

2. Where is ___ ___ dog?

High-Frequency Words: Stories and Activities • EMC 3376 • © Evan-Moor Corp.

# Read Naming Words

Look and read.

| ball | box | car |

Draw lines to match the words with the pictures.

1. box •

• 

2. car •

• 

3. ball •

• 

Read and color.

I see a red ball.

I see a blue car.

I see a yellow box.

Name

Read the poem out loud.
Color the ball, the car, and the box.

# Red, Blue, Yellow

Where is my red ball,
    my red ball, my red ball?
Where is my red ball?
Find my red ball for me.

Where is my blue car,
    my blue car, my blue car?
Where is my blue car?
Find my blue car for me.

Where is my yellow box,
    my yellow box, my yellow box?
Where is my yellow box?
Find my yellow box for me.

High-Frequency Words: Stories and Activities • EMC 3376 • © Evan-Moor Corp.

Note: Follow the directions on page 5.

# Get Ready, Get Set, Read!

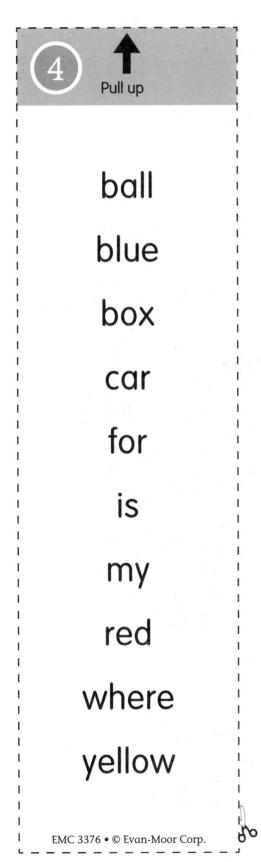

④ Pull up

ball

blue

box

car

for

is

my

red

where

yellow

EMC 3376 • © Evan-Moor Corp.

④

**Red, Blue, Yellow**

**WOW!**
I can read these words!

_____
Name

High-Frequency Words: Stories and Activities
EMC 3376 • © Evan-Moor Corp.

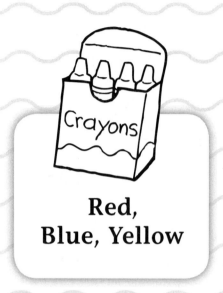

**Red,
Blue, Yellow**

High-Frequency Words: Stories and Activities • EMC 3376 • © Evan-Moor Corp.

# Learn New Words

Trace and write.

Read each word.

| and | funny | it |
| make | one | it three |

# Practice New Words

Draw lines to match the words.

and •                    • funny

funny •                  • one

it •                     • and

one •                    • it

make •                   • three

three •                  • make

Trace and write. Use a word from above.

one, two, _ _ _ _ _ _

# Read Naming Words

Look and read.

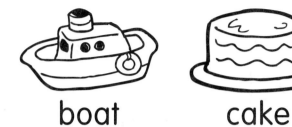

boat        cake        cat

Draw a line to the missing word.

1. I see a funny _____.

      •                    • cat

2. I see a funny _____.

      •                    • boat

3. I see a funny _____.

      •                    • cake

Draw a funny cat. Then read the sentence.

I see a funny cat.

Read the poem out loud.
Circle what is funny to you.

# I Can Make It!

I can make a funny boat.
A funny boat for you and me.
I can make it one, two, three!

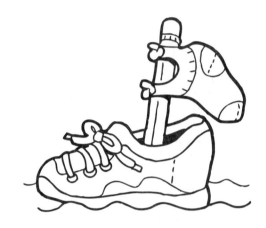

I can make a funny cake.
A funny cake for you and me.
I can make it one, two, three!

I can make a funny cat.
A funny cat for you and me.
I can make it one, two, three!

Note: Follow the directions on page 5.

# Get Ready, Get Set, Read!

(5) ↑ Pull up

and

boat

cake

cat

funny

it

make

one

three

EMC 3376 • © Evan-Moor Corp.

(5)

## I Can Make It!

**WOW!**
I can read these words!

_____
Name

High-Frequency Words: Stories and Activities
EMC 3376 • © Evan-Moor Corp.

# I Can Make It!

Name _____

Color a star for every word you read. Write how many.

## I Can Read!

☆ A
☆ a
☆ and
☆ away
☆ big
☆ blue
☆ can
☆ come
☆ down
☆ find
☆ for
☆ funny
☆ go
☆ help
☆ I
☆ in
☆ is

I can read ____ words.

fold

## I Can Read!

☆ it
☆ little
☆ look
☆ make
☆ me
☆ my
☆ not
☆ one
☆ red
☆ see
☆ the
☆ three
☆ two
☆ up
☆ where
☆ yellow
☆ you

I can read ____ words.

High-Frequency Words: Stories and Activities • EMC 3376 • © Evan-Moor Corp.

# Learn New Words

Trace and write.

jump

play

run

said

to

we

Read each word.

| jump | play | run |
|------|------|-----|
| said | to | we |

# Practice New Words

Circle the words that are the same as the first word in each row.

| 1. jump | jump | jump | bump |
|---------|------|------|------|
| 2. said | sad | said | said |
| 3. to | to | too | to |
| 4. run | ran | run | run |
| 5. we | we | we | web |
| 6. play | pay | play | play |

Look at the picture. Write the missing word.

I play and I ___ ___ ___ ___.

# Read Naming Words

Look and read.

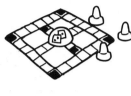        

game        pig        rabbit

Match each sentence to a word.

1. It can jump.        •    • pig

2. It is big.        •    • game

3. It is fun.        •    • rabbit

Circle the word that completes each sentence.

1. We see the (**pig**, **big**) run.

2. Look at the (**rabbit**, **rat**) jump!

3. I said, "We can play a (**come**, **game**)."

Read the story out loud.
Then jump like Pig and Rabbit.

# Jump and Run

Pig said to Rabbit,

"I can jump.

You can run.

We can play a game."

Rabbit said to Pig,

"You can jump.

I can run.

We can play a game."

Pig and Rabbit said,

"We can jump.

We can run.

We can play a game."

High-Frequency Words: Stories and Activities • EMC 3376 • © Evan-Moor Corp.

Note: Follow the directions on page 5.

# Get Ready, Get Set, Read!

**6** ↑ Pull up

game

jump

pig

play

rabbit

run

said

to

we

EMC 3376 • © Evan-Moor Corp.

**6**

## Jump and Run

**WOW!** I can read these words!

_____
Name

High-Frequency Words: Stories and Activities
EMC 3376 • © Evan-Moor Corp.

# Jump and Run

# Learn New Words

Trace and write.

brown

do

like

ride

under

what

Read each word.

| | | |
|---|---|---|
| brown | do | like |
| ride | under | what |

# Practice New Words

Connect to make a match.

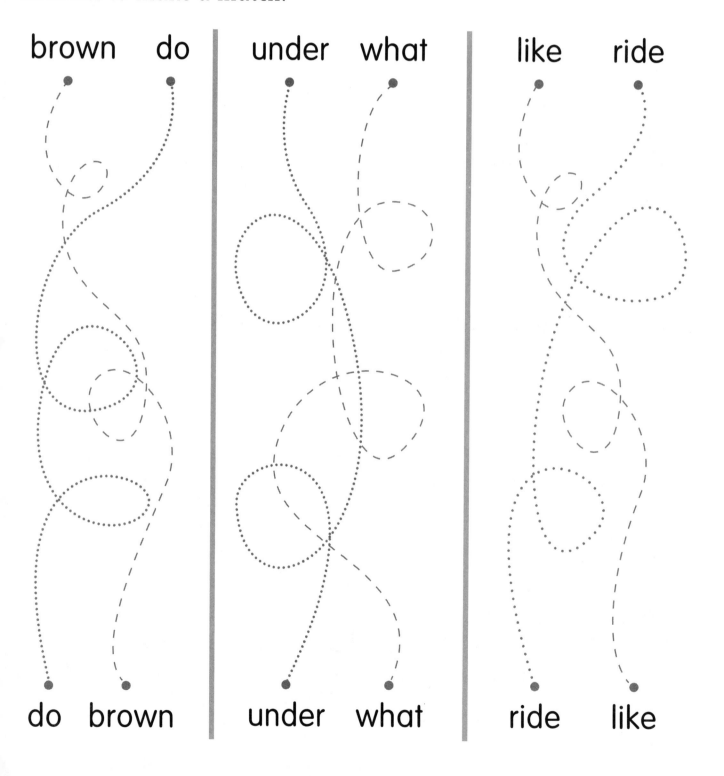

brown     do       under     what       like     ride

do     brown       under     what       ride     like

High-Frequency Words: Stories and Activities • EMC 3376 • © Evan-Moor Corp.

# Read Naming Words

Draw a line to the missing word.

1. The _____ is hot. •

•
   horse

2. The apple is under the _____. •

•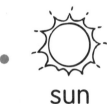
   sun

3. Do you like to ride a _____? •

•
   tree

---

Circle all that can be true in each row.

1. It can run.          horse     sun     tree

2. It is brown.         horse     sun     tree

3. You can ride it.     horse     sun     tree

4. It is big.           horse     sun     tree

Name

Read the story out loud.
Tell what you like to do.

# Ride in the Sun

I like to ride.

I ride a brown horse.

We ride under a tree.

What do you like?

I like to ride.

I ride a brown horse.

We go up and down.

What do you like?

I like to ride.

I ride a brown horse.

We ride under the sun.

What do you like?

High-Frequency Words: Stories and Activities • EMC 3376 • © Evan-Moor Corp.

Note: Follow the directions on page 5.

# Get Ready, Get Set, Read!

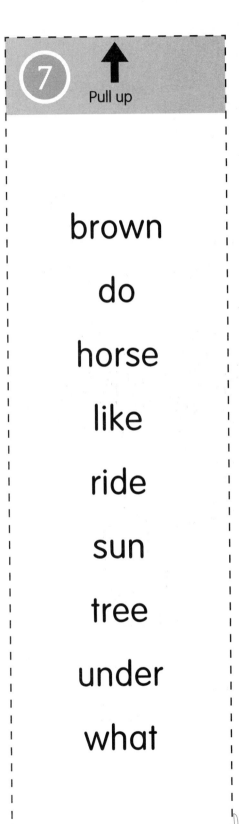

(7) ⬆ Pull up

brown

do

horse

like

ride

sun

tree

under

what

(7)

## Ride in the Sun

**WOW!**
I can read these words!

_____
Name

High-Frequency Words: Stories and Activities
EMC 3376 • © Evan-Moor Corp.

# Ride
# in the Sun

# Learn New Words

Trace and write.

am

at

here

new

soon

too

will

Read each word.

| am | at | here | new |
| soon | too | will |

# Practice New Words

Are the words the same? Color the face.

|  |  |  | yes | no |
|---|---|---|---|---|
| 1. | too | top | ☺ | ☹ |
| 2. | will | will | ☺ | ☹ |
| 3. | here | here | ☺ | ☹ |
| 4. | at | ate | ☺ | ☹ |
| 5. | am | am | ☺ | ☹ |
| 6. | new | new | ☺ | ☹ |
| 7. | soon | soon | ☺ | ☹ |

Complete each sentence. Use the words in the box.

soon    new

1. I will see you ___ ___ ___ .

2. Here is a ___ ___ ___ game.

# Read Naming Words

Look and read.

cow          farm          horse          pig

Match each sentence to a word.

1. What is at the farm?  •                    • a pig

2. What is at the farm?  •                    • a cow

3. What is at the farm?  •                    • a horse

Draw what is at the farm.

Read the story out loud.
Draw a cow.

# At the Farm

I am at a farm.
I like it here.

The farm is fun.
I run and play.
I am a helper, too.

A horse is here.
A new pig is here, too.
A new cow will come soon.

I like it at the farm.
Come and see me soon.
You will like it here, too.

Note: Follow the directions on page 5.

# Get Ready, Get Set, Read!

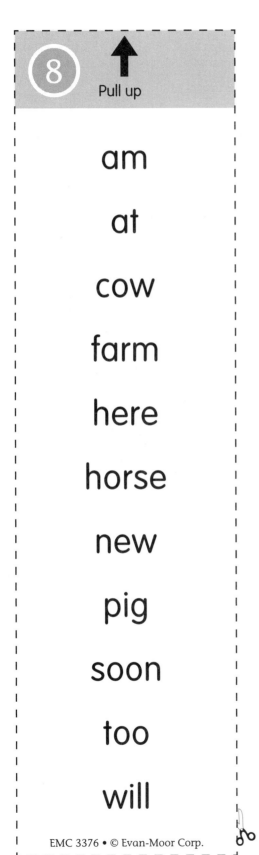

(8) ↑ Pull up

am

at

cow

farm

here

horse

new

pig

soon

too

will

EMC 3376 • © Evan-Moor Corp.

(8)

**At the Farm**

**Wow!** I can read these words!

_____
Name

High-Frequency Words: Stories and Activities
EMC 3376 • © Evan-Moor Corp.

## At the Farm

High-Frequency Words: Stories and Activities • EMC 3376 • © Evan-Moor Corp.

# Learn New Words

Trace and write.

all

ate

eat

good

have

must

want

Read each word.

| all | ate | eat | good |
|-----|-----|-----|------|
| have | must | want | |

# Practice New Words

Draw lines to match the words.

| | |
|---|---|
| ate • | • good |
| must • | • all |
| all • | • have |
| want • | • eat |
| have • | • ate |
| good • | • want |
| eat • | • must |

Circle the word that completes each sentence.

1. I want to (**eat**, **ate**) the apple.

2. I (**all**, **ate**) a good apple.

# Read Naming Words

Look and read.

**cake**

**milk**

---

Circle the pictures that go with each word.

1. cake

2. milk

---

Complete the sentences. Use the words above.

1. I ate all of the _____ _____ _____ _____.

2. Do you want some _____ _____ _____ _____?

Read the story out loud.
Draw what you like to eat.

# I Eat Cake

I want to eat cake.
I must have cake!
Cake is good to eat.

I want to have milk.
I must have milk!
Milk is good.

I ate it all.
I ate all the cake.

I like cake and milk.
Do you?

High-Frequency Words: Stories and Activities • EMC 3376 • © Evan-Moor Corp.

# Get Ready, Get Set, Read!

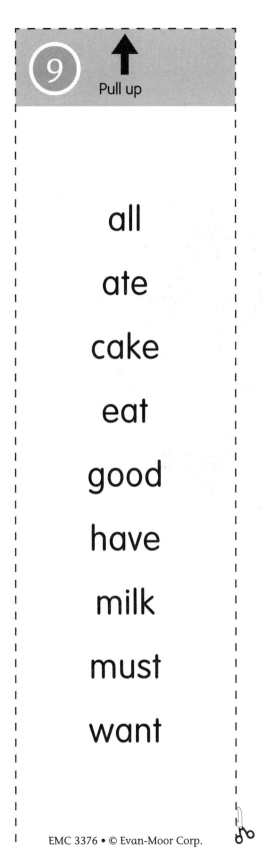

(9) ↑ Pull up

all

ate

cake

eat

good

have

milk

must

want

EMC 3376 • © Evan-Moor Corp.

(9)

**I Eat Cake**

WOW! I can read these words!

Name

High-Frequency Words: Stories and Activities
EMC 3376 • © Evan-Moor Corp.

## I Eat Cake

# Learn New Words

Trace and write.

came

did

get

into

there

this

Read each word.

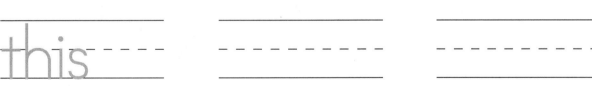

| came | did | get |
|------|------|------|
| into | there | this |

# Practice New Words

Connect to make a match.

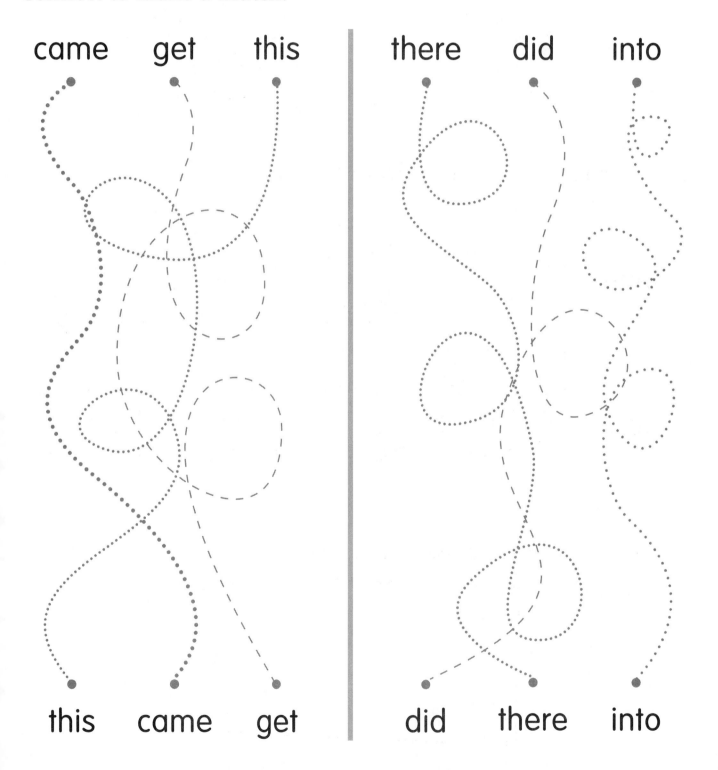

came     get     this        there     did     into

this     came     get        did     there     into

# Read Naming Words

Look and read.

box

letter

---

Circle the pictures that go with each word.

1. letter

---

2. box

---

Did you get a letter? Write your name.

Read the poem out loud.
Who got a letter? Point.

# A Letter for Me

Did I get a letter?

Is there a letter for me?

Look into the box.

What do you see?


A letter came for me!

This is my letter!

This letter came for me!


Did you get a letter?

Did you get a letter, too?

Look into the box.

Is there a letter for you?

Note: Follow the directions on page 5.

# Get Ready, Get Set, Read!

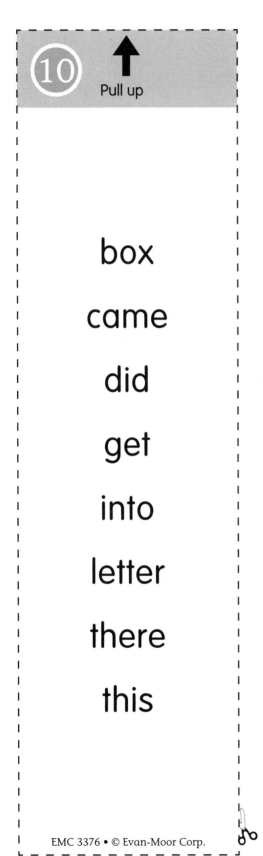

(10) ↑ Pull up

box

came

did

get

into

letter

there

this

EMC 3376 • © Evan-Moor Corp.

(10)

**A Letter for Me**

Mr. Ben Wheeler
519 Winter Street
Miami, FL 43333

**WOW!**
I can read these words!

_____
Name

High-Frequency Words: Stories and Activities
EMC 3376 • © Evan-Moor Corp.

## A Letter for Me

Name _____

Color a star for every word you read. Write how many.

## I Can Read!

☆ all
☆ am
☆ at
☆ ate
☆ brown
☆ came
☆ did
☆ do
☆ eat
☆ get
☆ good
☆ have
☆ here
☆ into
☆ jump
☆ like

I can read ____ words.

fold

## I Can Read!

☆ must
☆ new
☆ play
☆ ride
☆ run
☆ said
☆ soon
☆ there
☆ this
☆ to
☆ too
☆ under
☆ want
☆ we
☆ what
☆ will

I can read ____ words.

# Learn New Words

Trace and write.

but

four

now

say

they

was

who

Read each word.

| but | four | now | say |
|-----|------|-----|-----|
| | they | was | who | |

# Practice New Words

Are the words the same? Color the face.

|   |   |   | yes | no |
|---|---|---|---|---|
| 1. | four | find | ☺ | ☹ |
| 2. | now | new | ☺ | ☹ |
| 3. | was | was | ☺ | ☹ |
| 4. | who | who | ☺ | ☹ |
| 5. | but | bat | ☺ | ☹ |
| 6. | they | try | ☺ | ☹ |
| 7. | say | say | ☺ | ☹ |

Complete the sentences. Use the words in the box.

> four   was

1. I ___ ___ ___ three.

2. But now I am ___ ___ ___ ___.

# Read Naming Words

Look and read.

birthday

sister

Draw lines to match the words with the pictures.

1. birthday •

2. sister •

Circle the word that completes each sentence.

1. I have a big (**said**, **sister**).

2. They say my (**see**, **sister**) is four.

3. I like (**birthday**, **birth**) cake.

Read the poem out loud.
Draw four birthday hats.

# Now I Am Four

Who is three?

I was three.

But this is my birthday.

Now I am four.

Did they say I was three?

Who is three?

My sister is three.

But not me.

This is my birthday.

Now I am four.

Did they say I was three?

My sister is three.

But not me!

High-Frequency Words: Stories and Activities • EMC 3376 • © Evan-Moor Corp.

Note: Follow the directions on page 5.

# Get Ready, Get Set, Read!

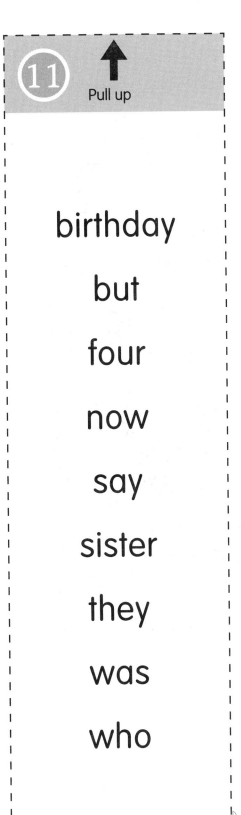

(11) ↑ Pull up

birthday

but

four

now

say

sister

they

was

who

EMC 3376 • © Evan-Moor Corp.

(11)

## Now I Am Four

**WOW!**

I can read these words!

Name

High-Frequency Words: Stories and Activities
EMC 3376 • © Evan-Moor Corp.

# Now I Am Four

# Learn New Words

Trace and write.

black

gray

hi

on

our

out

white

Read each word.

| black | gray | hi | on |
|-------|------|-----|-----|
| our | out | white | |

# Practice New Words

Circle the words that are the same as the first word in each row.

| 1. out | out | out | at |
| 2. black | back | black | black |
| 3. gray | play | gray | gray |
| 4. hi | hi | hi | hip |
| 5. our | our | out | our |
| 6. on | an | on | on |
| 7. white | white | write | white |

Look at the picture. Write a color word from above.

Hi, black and __ __ __ __ __ cat.

# Read Naming Words

Draw a line to the missing word.

1. I like to look out our _____.  •                    •

duck

2. A _____ is a bird.  •                    •

cat

3. My ball is on the _____.  •                    •

window

4. A _____ can jump.  •                    •

grass

Circle all that can be true in each row.

| | cat | duck | grass |
|---|---|---|---|
| 1. It can eat grass. | cat | duck | grass |
| 2. It can run. | cat | duck | grass |
| 3. You can play on it. | cat | duck | grass |
| 4. You can play with it. | cat | duck | grass |

Read the story out loud.
Color the cat, the duck, and the rabbit.

# Our Window

I look out our window.

I see a black cat.

The cat is on the grass.

Hi, black cat!

I look out our window.

I see a white duck.

The duck is on the grass.

Hi, white duck!

I look out our window.

I see a gray rabbit.

The rabbit is on the grass.

Hi, gray rabbit!

High-Frequency Words: Stories and Activities • EMC 3376 • © Evan-Moor Corp.

Note: Follow the directions on page 5.

# Get Ready, Get Set, Read!

## Our Window

High-Frequency Words: Stories and Activities • EMC 3376 • © Evan-Moor Corp.

# Learn New Words

Trace and write.

he

pink

purple

saw

she

that

with

Read each word.

| he | pink | purple | saw |
|----|------|--------|-----|
| | she | that | with |

# Practice New Words

Draw lines to match the words.

purple •                    • that

with •                      • pink

saw •                       • he

that •                      • with

she •                       • purple

he •                        • saw

pink •                      • she

Write a color word from above. Then color the pig.

She saw a _____ pig.

# Read Naming Words

Look and read.

cat            eye            eyes            fish

Draw a line to the missing word.

1. You have two _____ to see.  •          • cat

2. My cat will eat a _____.  •          • eye

3. He saw a _____ in a tree.  •          • eyes

4. That _____ is blue.  •          • fish

Draw what the cat is missing.
Write the word.

_____ _____ _____ _____

Read the story out loud.
Color the eyes of the cat and the fish.

# What They Saw

She saw a cat with funny eyes.

One eye was pink.

One eye was purple.

That is the cat she saw.

He saw a fish with funny eyes.

One eye was purple.

One eye was pink.

That is the fish he saw.

She saw a funny cat.

He saw a funny fish.

That is what they saw.

Fish Food

High-Frequency Words: Stories and Activities • EMC 3376 • © Evan-Moor Corp.

Note: Follow the directions on page 5.

# Get Ready, Get Set, Read!

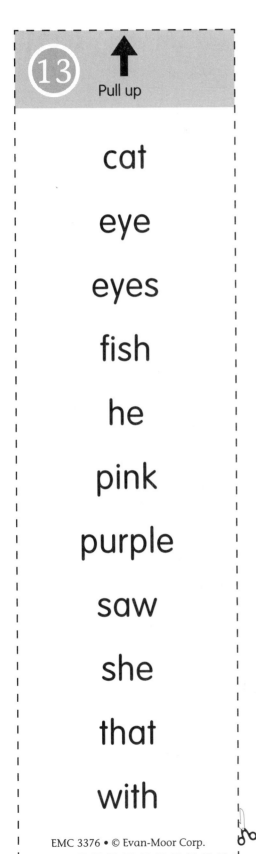

**(13)** ↑ Pull up

cat

eye

eyes

fish

he

pink

purple

saw

she

that

with

**13**

## What They Saw

**WOW!** I can read these words!

_____
Name

# What They Saw

High-Frequency Words: Stories and Activities • EMC 3376 • © Evan-Moor Corp.

# Learn New Words

Trace and write.

are

good-bye

green

hello

orange

pretty

so

Read each word.

| are | good-bye | green | hello |
|-----|----------|-------|-------|
| orange | pretty | so |  |

# Practice New Words

Are the words the same? Color the face.

|   |   |   | yes | no |
|---|---|---|-----|-----|
| 1. | are | are | ☺ | ☹ |
| 2. | green | green | ☺ | ☹ |
| 3. | so | see | ☺ | ☹ |
| 4. | good-bye | good-bye | ☺ | ☹ |
| 5. | hello | hill | ☺ | ☹ |
| 6. | one | orange | ☺ | ☹ |
| 7. | pretty | pretty | ☺ | ☹ |

Complete the sentences. Use the words in the box.

> hello   are

1. My eyes ___ ___ ___ so pretty!

2. I said ___ ___ ___ ___ ___ to Matt.

# Read Naming Words

Draw a line to the missing word.

1. You have two _____ to see. • •  back

2. I have two _____ to jump. • •  eyes

3. My green eyes are in my _____. • •  legs

4. I can not see my _____. • •  head

Circle all that can be true in each row.

1. They help you run.　eyes　head　legs

2. They help you see.　eyes　head　legs

3. You have two.　eyes　head　legs

4. You have one.　eyes　head　legs

Read the story out loud.
Color the bird.

# Hello, Pretty Bird

My back is green.

My legs are orange.

See my back.

See my legs.

I am so pretty!

My eyes are green.

My head is orange.

See my eyes.

See my head.

I am so pretty!

I can say hello.

And I can say good-bye.

Good-bye!

Note: Follow the directions on page 5.

# Get Ready, Get Set, Read!

(14) ↑ Pull up

are

back

eyes

good-bye

green

head

hello

legs

orange

pretty

so

EMC 3376 • © Evan-Moor Corp.

(14)

## Hello, Pretty Bird

**Wow!** I can read these words!

_____
Name

High-Frequency Words: Stories and Activities
EMC 3376 • © Evan-Moor Corp.

# Hello, Pretty
# Bird

# Learn New Words

Trace and write.

be

no

please

ran

well

went

yes

Read each word.

| be | no | please | ran |
|----|----|--------|-----|
| well | went | yes | |

# Practice New Words

Connect to make a match.

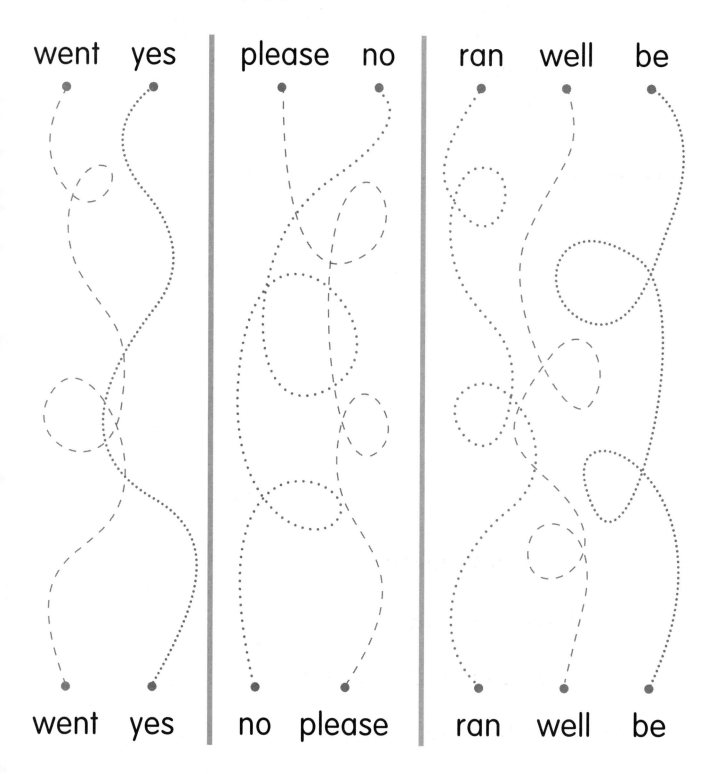

went    yes        please    no        ran    well    be

went    yes        no    please        ran    well    be

# Read Naming Words

Look and read.

bed

hand

Draw lines to match the words with the pictures.

**1.** bed •

**2.** hand •

Circle the word that completes each sentence.

**1.** Yes, I like my big (**bug**, **bed**).

**2.** No, the ball is not in my (**here**, **hand**).

**3.** They ran to (**bed**, **red**).

Read the poem out loud.
Draw what went to bed on Papa's head.

# It Ran in Here

Well, where can it be?

Here is my hand.

Please look with me.

Is it in here? No.

Is it in there? No.

Well, where can it be?

Here is my hand.

Please look with me.

Is it in here? Yes!

Yes! It ran in here.

It ran in here.

It went to bed.

It went to bed on Papa's head!

    High-Frequency Words: Stories and Activities • EMC 3376 • © Evan-Moor Corp.

Note: Follow the directions on page 5.

# Get Ready, Get Set, Read!

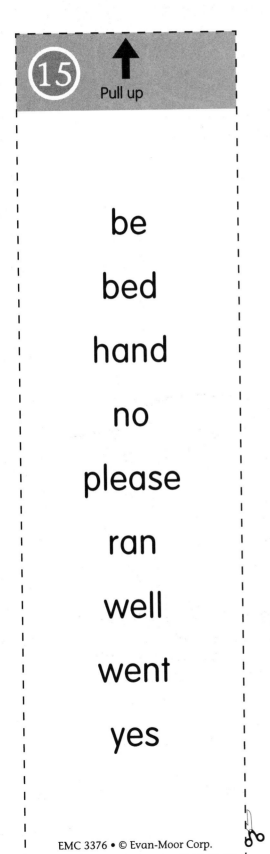

(15) ↑ Pull up

be

bed

hand

no

please

ran

well

went

yes

15

## It Ran in Here

WOW!
I can read these words!

_____
Name

# It Ran in Here

High-Frequency Words: Stories and Activities • EMC 3376 • © Evan-Moor Corp.

Name _____

Color a star for every word you read. Write how many.

## I Can Read!

⭐ are
⭐ be
⭐ black
⭐ but
⭐ four
⭐ good-bye
⭐ gray
⭐ green
⭐ he
⭐ hello
⭐ hi
⭐ no
⭐ now
⭐ on
⭐ orange
⭐ our
⭐ out
⭐ pink

I can read ____ words.

fold

## I Can Read!

⭐ please
⭐ pretty
⭐ purple
⭐ ran
⭐ saw
⭐ say
⭐ she
⭐ so
⭐ that
⭐ they
⭐ was
⭐ well
⭐ went
⭐ white
⭐ who
⭐ with
⭐ yes

I can read ____ words.

YOU ARE A STAR!

I can read 100 sight words!

_____
Name

High-Frequency Words: Stories and Activities • EMC 3376 • © Evan-Moor Corp.

# Answer Key

## Page 10

## Page 11

## Page 16

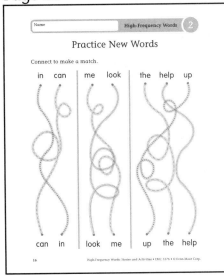

## Page 17

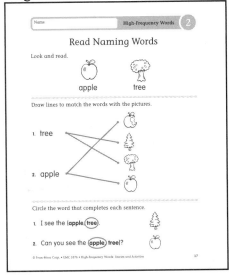

## Page 22

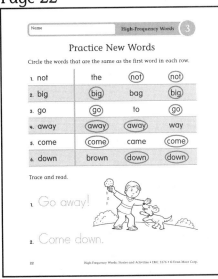

## Page 23

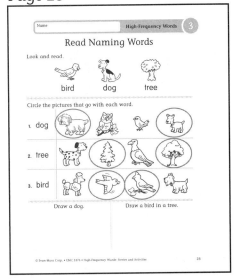

## Page 28

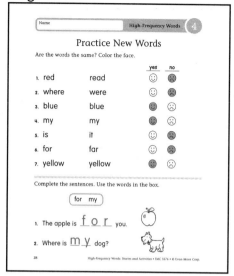

## Page 29

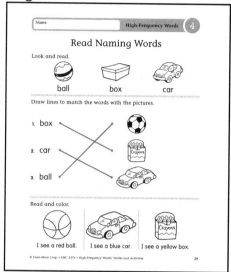

## Page 34

## Page 35

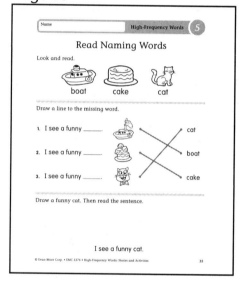

## Page 42

## Page 43

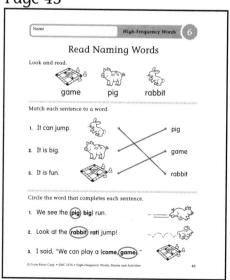

High-Frequency Words: Stories and Activities • EMC 3376 • © Evan-Moor Corp.

## Page 48

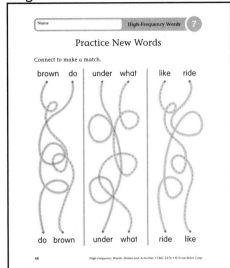

## Page 49

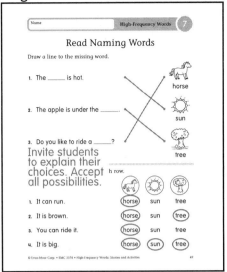

## Page 54

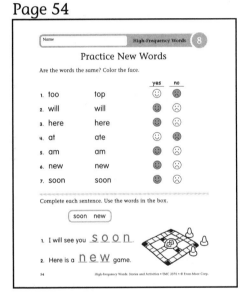

## Page 55

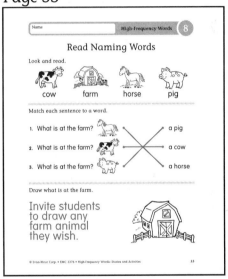

## Page 60

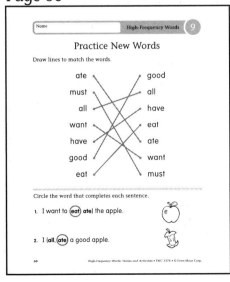

## Page 61

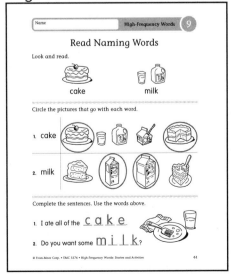

**Page 66**

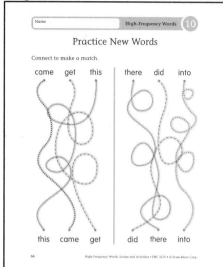

**Page 67**

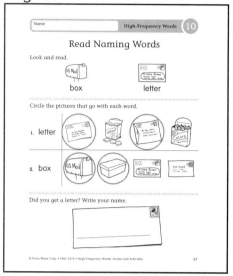

**Page 74**

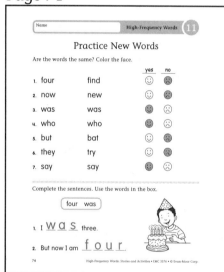

**Page 75**

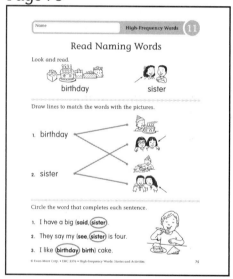

**Page 80**

**Page 81**

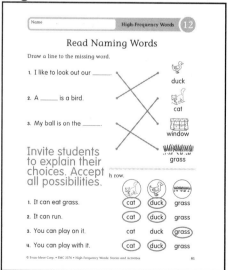

## Page 86

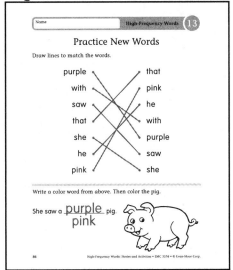

**Practice New Words**

Draw lines to match the words.

purple — with
with — purple
saw — she
that — he
she — saw
he — that
pink — pink

Write a color word from above. Then color the pig.

She saw a ~~purple~~ pink pig.

## Page 87

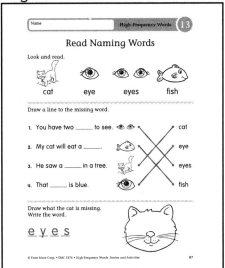

**Read Naming Words**

Look and read.

cat   eye   eyes   fish

Draw a line to the missing word.

1. You have two _____ to see. — eyes
2. My cat will eat a _____. — fish
3. He saw a _____ in a tree. — cat
4. That _____ is blue. — eye

Draw what the cat is missing.
Write the word.

e y e s

## Page 92

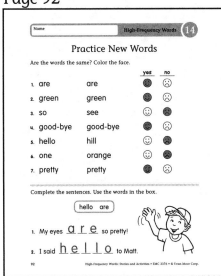

**Practice New Words**

Are the words the same? Color the face.

| | | yes | no |
|---|---|---|---|
| 1. | are — are | ☺ | ☹ |
| 2. | green — green | ☺ | ☹ |
| 3. | so — see | ☺ | ☹ |
| 4. | good-bye — good-bye | ☺ | ☹ |
| 5. | hello — hill | ☺ | ☹ |
| 6. | one — orange | ☺ | ☹ |
| 7. | pretty — pretty | ☺ | ☹ |

Complete the sentences. Use the words in the box.

hello   are

1. My eyes a r e so pretty!
2. I said h e l l o to Matt.

## Page 93

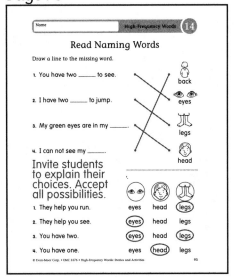

**Read Naming Words**

Draw a line to the missing word.

1. You have two _____ to see. — back
2. I have two _____ to jump. — eyes
3. My green eyes are in my _____. — legs
4. I can not see my _____. — head

Invite students to explain their choices. Accept all possibilities.

1. They help you run. — eyes   head   (legs)
2. They help you see. — (eyes)   head   legs
3. You have two. — (eyes)   head   (legs)
4. You have one. — eyes   (head)   legs

## Page 98

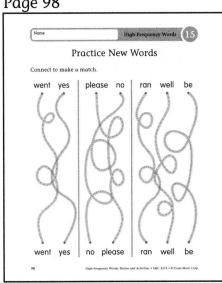

**Practice New Words**

Connect to make a match.

went   yes | please   no | ran   well   be

went   yes | no   please | ran   well   be

## Page 99

**Read Naming Words**

Look and read.

bed   hand

Draw lines to match the words with the pictures.

1. bed
2. hand

Circle the word that completes each sentence.

1. Yes, I like my big (bug, **bed**).
2. No, the ball is not in my (here, **hand**).
3. They ran to (**bed**, red).

# Evan-Moor's Read and Understand

The **Read and Understand** series provides teachers with a comprehensive resource of stories and skills pages to supplement any core reading program. Use as directed lessons or independent practice.

## Read and Understand Stories and Activities

Resource books containing reproducible stories and practice materials for a wide spectrum of reading skills. More than 20 stories included, with fun illustrations. An answer key is provided. 144 pages. **Correlated to state standards.**

| | | | |
|---|---|---|---|
| **Grade K** | EMC 637 | **Grade 3** | EMC 640 |
| **Grade 1** | EMC 638 | **Grades 4–6+, Fiction** | EMC 748 |
| **Grade 2** | EMC 639 | **Grades 4–6+, Nonfiction** | EMC 749 |

## More Read and Understand Stories and Activities

Provides teachers with a comprehensive resource of stories and skills pages to supplement any core reading program. The practice activities following each story include a comprehension page, a vocabulary page, and a phonics or structural analysis page. 144 pages. **Correlated to state standards.**

| | |
|---|---|
| **Grade 1** | EMC 745 |
| **Grade 2** | EMC 746 |
| **Grade 3** | EMC 747 |